FRUIT OF THE SPIRIT

PATIENCE

Fruit of the Spirit Study Guide Series

Love

Joy

Peace

Patience

Kindness

Goodness

Faithfulness

Gentleness

Self-Control

CALVIN MILLER

 FRUIT OF THE SPIRIT

PATIENCE

Published in Nashville, Tennessee, by Thomas Nelson. Thomas Nelson is a trademark of Thomas Nelson, Inc.

Typesetting by Gregory C. Benoit Publishing, Old Mystic, CT

Thomas Nelson, Inc., titles may be purchased in bulk for educational, business, fund-raising, or sales promotional use. For information, please e-mail SpecialMarkets@ThomasNelson.com.

Unless otherwise noted, Scripture quotations are taken from the HOLY BIBLE: NEW INTERNATIONAL VERSION®. Copyright © 1973, 1978, 1984 by International Bible Society. Used by permission of Zondervan. All rights reserved.

Scripture quotations marked TLB are taken from *The Living Bible*. © 1971. Used by permission of Tyndale House Publishers, Inc., Wheaton, Illinois 60189. All rights reserved.

ISBN: 978-1-4185-2836-2

Printed in the United States of America
08 09 10 11 12 RRD 9 8 7 6 5 4 3 2 1

TABLE OF CONTENTS

But the fruit of the Spirit is love, joy, peace, patience, kindness, goodness, faithfulness, gentleness and self-control. Against such things there is no law.
—Galatians 5:22–23

INTRODUCTION

We've heard it said that "patience is a virtue," and, according to the dictionary, a virtue is a "quality of good in human conduct." The world says that we learn to be patient; the Bible says patience is a gift of the Holy Spirit.

Patience is a direct result of God's Spirit in us. Therefore, we need to focus more on giving the Holy Spirit control of our lives than on developing specific characteristics.

This study isn't about learning to be patient; it's about learning to give control of our lives to God. The more we do that, the more we will see his character come alive in us. Patience isn't something we develop; it is something God develops in us as he takes over.

But patience is more than something we need when traffic backs up or we are sitting in a doctor's office. Patience is something that sustains us while we wait for God's will to be revealed. Patience reminds us that God's timing is not our timing. Patience is quiet confidence in God's promised provision.

In the fifth chapter of Galatians, Paul set in opposition the works of the flesh and the fruit of the Spirit. The works of the flesh are self-destructive and do nothing positive for a person's relationships with other people. The fruits of the Spirit, however, are beneficial to individuals and the faith community. Patience, therefore, is good for you and for those with whom you interact.

What does patience look like? It looks like God standing on the eastern shore of the Red Sea waiting for Israel to take that step of faith. It looks like the loving father awaiting the return of the prodigal son. It looks like Jesus Christ standing at the door and knocking. Patience is yielding to God's perception of our circumstances in light of his view of the future.

Throughout our lives, God has demonstrated incredible patience with us. He has loved us when we weren't very lovable and provided for us when we weren't very grateful. He has reassured us in our times of doubt and held us together in our times of grief and pain. He has been patient while waiting for us to abandon our selfish ways in favor of obedience to him.

God doesn't know how to be patient; he *is* patience. His very essence is love and kindness, justice, and patience. And it is that patience that he brings into our lives when we invite him to live inside of us.

In today's world where being hurried is normal, we need God's kind of patience. In this study, you will discover that God's patience is available to those who desire it because, as Paul said, there is no law against it (Galatians 5:23).

HOW TO USE THIS GUIDE

Galatians 5:22–23 is not a plan to achieve better faith. Rather, it is a description of God's personal gifts to all of us. If we follow God and seek his blessing, then the fruits of the Spirit are a natural overflow in our relationship with God. We are to grow in character so that one day we will reflect the image of our Lord.

This series of nine six-week studies will clearly focus your spiritual life to become more like Christ. Each study guide is divided into six weeks, and each of the six-week courses covers one of the fruits of the Spirit. Participants simply read each daily study and answer the questions at the end of each devotional. This prepares everyone for the group discussion at the end of the week.

Each week features a similar pattern that explores one aspect of that study's fruit of the Spirit. The first lesson establishes the aspect of the fruit to be explored throughout the week. The second lesson looks at the week's theme as it relates to God's purpose in the life of the believer. The third lesson looks at the week's theme as it relates to the believer's relationship with Christ. The fourth lesson explores how the fruit is relevant in service to others. And in the fifth lesson, the theme is related to personal worship. A sixth lesson is included as a bonus study, and focuses on either a biblical character who modeled this particular fruit, or a key parable that brings the theme into focus.

Each weeklong study should conclude in a group review. The weekly group discussion serves as a place to understand the practical side of the theme and receive encouragement and feedback on the journey to become more Christlike. For the study to have the character-transforming effect God desires, it is important for the participant to spend ten to twenty minutes a day reading the Scripture passage and the devotional, and to think through the two questions for the day. If each participant reads all of the questions beforehand, it greatly enhances the group dynamic. Each participant should choose three or four questions to discuss during the group session.

These simple guidelines will help make group time productive. Take a total of about forty-five minutes to answer and discuss the questions. Each person need not answer every question, but be sure all members participate. You can stimulate participation by having everyone respond to an icebreaker question. Have each group member answer the first of the six questions listed at the end of the week, and leave the remaining questions open-ended. Or, make up your own icebreaker question, such as: What color best represents the day you are having? What is your favorite movie? Or, how old were you when you had your first kiss?

No one should respond to all of the questions. Keep in mind that if you are always talking, the others are not. It is essential that everyone contribute. If you notice that someone is not participating, ask that group member which question is the most relevant. Be sensitive if something is keeping that member from contributing. Don't ask someone to read or pray aloud unless you know that the member is comfortable with such a task.

Always start and end your time with prayer. Sometimes it helps to have each person say what he or she plans to do with the lesson that week. Remember to reserve ten minutes for group prayer. You might want to keep a list of requests and answers to prayer at the back of this book.

Week 1: The Art of Waiting on God

Memory Passage for the Week: Psalm 37:3–4

Day 1: The Art of Waiting on God

God's clocks have no second hands. His days are millennia. Alarm clocks are insignificant in heaven. 2 Peter 3:8–9.

Day 2: The Purpose of God in My Life

When we wait on God, he will put a new song in our hearts. Psalm 40:1–3.

Day 3: My Relationship with Christ

God cares for us; that is enough. Believing this is Christ's recipe for our own worry-free living. Matthew 6:25–27.

Day 4: My Service to Others

God is patient with us, even when we stray. In the same way, we should be patient with those who are lost. Exodus 23:9.

Day 5: My Personal Worship

The essence of arriving at a state of patience is the ability to take all our "inner noise," all our "initial, endless chatter," and order it to be quiet. Psalm 131:1–3.

Day 6: A Character Study on Noah

Genesis 6:1–21; 9:8–16

Day 7: Group Discussion

Day 1: The Art of Waiting on God
Read 2 Peter 3:8—9

In his brief but significant letter, Peter reminded us that impatience is a frequent problem in churches. God has a big clock; its slow-moving hands tick off the centuries. We have only small clocks whose twirling hands sweep past the hurried seconds of our lives. Time! Peter says in this passage that God's clocks have no second hands. His days are millennia. Alarm clocks are insignificant in heaven.

A thousand years are but a day, and with such a clock God never gets neurotic. There are no deadlines. God rules and there is no rush—speed and high velocity are only for those who wear watches and keep appointment books.

We are very concerned about seconds, minutes, and the like. But God, who is eternal, measures a thousand years as they are a day. In the stretch between our small, short lives and the never-ending life of God, we fidget and grow impatient. But if we move in close to God and dwell in his everlasting light, we shall find contentment without impatience.

There is a real art to patience.

The art consists of aligning our little watches with his immense clock. We do not have unlimited time to accomplish his plan for our lives. Therefore we must, as the psalmist suggests, "number our days" (Psalm 90:12). What does he mean by this? We are to never forget that our lives are finite and — especially by the reckoning of God's great clock—coming to a swift end. Therefore we must do two things. First, we must pace ourselves so that we do not live frantically, and then we must schedule the appointments of our lives so that every earthly moment yields some heavenly product.

Questions for Personal Reflection

1. What spiritual contribution are you making to your world right now?

2. When your life comes to an end, for what do you want to be remembered?

Day 2: The Purpose of God in My Life

Read Psalm 40:1–3

"Out of the pit, out of the mire" is the biography of every believer. There is a pit that creates in us a yearning for freedom. We long for God's joy and, above all, for his liberty. But the pit will not let us be free. This condition causes us to need. There God finds us, and we can believe in and celebrate the word *grace* because we know we did not—nor could we—extricate ourselves from the pit. We cry out for rescue simply because we know we are helpless. We wait for him. Floundering, floundering, floundering! Entrapped, ensnared, dying—we wait, and our patience is rewarded by the coming of our Rescuer. The Savior lifts us from the pit, and we are in love with him because he has saved us and endowed us with great liberty.

The poet in Psalm 40:1–3 felt entrenched in the mire. Circumstances, like quicksand, had grasped him and were dragging him down. He was trapped, and his liberty was void. The strongest thing about him was his desire to be free.

To fall into quicksand and live through it demands that the victim cease struggling. The law of escaping quicksand is "don't struggle." Lie back gently, fin with your hands, and let your calm be your rescuer. The same law will lift us from the slough of despond. The more we flail to achieve our own freedom, the more certain we are to be lost. But if we wait ... if we trust the Lord and wait ... our rescue is certain.

Questions for Personal Reflection

1. What spiritual advice would you give someone who is struggling in the pit of life?

2. In what ways are you living in the liberty of God's love? How does it affect your everyday life?

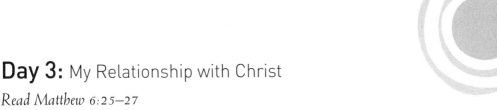

Day 3: My Relationship with Christ
Read Matthew 6:25–27

There is a scene in the Disney film *Bambi* where a group of animated hunters are walking through a field with guns, seeking to shoot a covey of animated quail. One of these fidgety birds is pacing nervously while a sister quail counsels her that she must not fly. But alas the fidgety quail is so nervous she bolts into the sky. There is a roar of shotgun fire from guns of the animated hunters and sadly, the poor quail is shot, and, in an explosion of animated feathers, she dies. She is not very animated after that.

The advice of this desperate, although fictional, quail is somehow like the birds in Jesus' sermon. There is great logic in living free of anxiety. Jesus' birds do not have psychiatrists. They are simply content to be what God made them to be … birds. God takes care of them and they need not worry. In all of God's nature, says Jesus in effect, neurotic birds do not exist.

Impatience is a deadly vice. Keeping calm can save an animated quail, but it can also keep us from hurrying into some poorly thought-out decision. When we make decisions in such haste, we can end up in a terrible situation or lifestyle—simply because we would not wait.

The dying quail in *Bambi* seems a bit violent for a children's story. Nonetheless, these animated birds do point to the lesson of the danger in letting our nerves get the best of us.

God created believers, and in their salvation, God gave them the grace to trust. God cares for us; it is enough. It is this trust—which even birds know—that is Christ's recipe for our own worry-free living.

Questions for Personal Reflection

1. Why is it so hard to trust God when facing uncertain times?

2. Think back on a time when you took matters into your own hands before turning to God. How would that situation have turned out had you first trusted God?

Day 4: My Service to Others
Read Exodus 23:9

We were all strangers to God at one time. We all needed others to save us. But now we are rescued and called by the Savior to go and rescue others. To be effective in our callings, we must not forget what it felt like to be an alien, a stranger. It has long been noted that those who are most recently born again are the most motivated to try and win others. Why? Probably because those newest in their salvation still remember what it was like to be lost.

Many times, those who have experienced little pain tend to inflict hurt on others. Those who exclude others from their social circles have rarely lived as an outcast. Cherish the times you have been lonely, for such times are your teachers. The lessons are painful, but they leave you more human. When you have hurt enough, you know you would never want another person to have to endure what you went through.

Here in Exodus, Moses counseled Israel to remember that for four hundred years they were exiles and foreigners in Egypt. Surely their four-century period of bondage had softened their hearts toward the strangers in their midst. If they remembered how they lived before God rescued them in the Exodus, surely they could feel compassion for all of those still living beyond the community of God!

Nobody wants to be an outcast; no one wants to be shut out. Everyone wants to be shut in to a close intimacy with Christ. *Inclusion* is a blessed word that really says all are welcome to enter the eternal embrace of God.

Questions for Personal Reflection

1. What hurts have you experienced in recent months?

2. How have those experiences changed the way you see others in similar situations?

Day 5: My Personal Worship
Read Psalm 131:1–3

In this psalm is the age-old quarrel of those who find their egos demand-ing that God set aside his majesty and pay attention to them. In all ego there is a writhing impatience—an impatience to have more glory, more recognition, and greater fame. The self-centered believer is marked by an unholy impatience that keeps him from seeing beyond his self-importance to the humbling glory of God.

David said, "I have stilled and quieted my soul" (Psalm 131:2). How did he do this? Like a mother weans her child, breaking the child from an infant diet, so David broke his ego from its diet of narcissism, the constant feeding on self-importance.

This is not as easy to do as one might think. The ego is a small inte-rior thing with an oversized mouth. Like a sparrow chick, ego keeps its beak turned up crying, "Feed me!"

"Feed you? With what?"

"Feed me with all I want, for I, your ego, cannot conceive of being happy with less than all I want. Oh yes! And did I mention I want it *now?* Not just enough—more than enough! Don't feed me; gorge me. Don't compliment me; flatter me! Don't give me a glass of wine; intoxi-cate me!"

Ego keeps shouting at us to do more, give more, and compliment more until the Holy Spirit moves in, teaching us the twin arts of temperance and patience.

Then ego at last takes its proper place.

Then ego is finally quiet—shut up by spiritual discipline. Then we can praise God freely without the ugly impediment of an impatient ego.

Questions for Personal Reflection

1. How does your ego affect your decisions and actions?

2. What are some ways you can control your ego?

Day 6: Noah—The Long Wait on the Promises of God

Read Genesis 6:1–21; 9:8–16

Patience is not just the ability to keep from hurrying. Patience is a will-
ingness to surrender your private agenda and proceed on God's timetable
at the exact pace he ordained for you. Noah was given an assignment to
build a huge seagoing vessel, and he was told that the entire construc-
tion crew would be his family. Obviously this was not an assignment that
could be accomplished quickly. It would be like giving a hammer and
saw to a British worker in the Southampton shipyards and saying, "Go
thou and build the *Queen Mary*." It would take him immeasurable years.
Noah likely did not know how long it would take, but he did know that
it would not be instantaneous.

The story is too sketchy to know how Noah dealt with the short-
term aspects of his long-term calling. But patience is not patience if it
frets over any amount of time. Patience rises each day, picks up its hammer and saw, faces the heavens, and says, "God, this day is yours. I may
not finish the ship before lunch, but I will drive each nail on schedule."

Patience holds no resentment. It never forgets that the finished product will be a boat built God's way on God's time. The best masons in history never merely cut stones, they built cathedrals. What if the cathedral
is still unfinished when they die? Never mind, they already trained their
apprentices. To these they pass on their vision. Those who follow them

must never waste a day merely chipping granite. Every moment must serve the final dream.

Noah found grace in the eyes of the Lord. He served God's dream. He was a good steward of every second. He was never neurotic about a single moment, for every moment worked toward the finished plan of God. The boat would be done when God said so, and each day for 120 years, Noah focused on God's ultimate finished product. In the meantime he dabbed the tar, sawed the timbers, and looked to heaven. He saved his life one confident day at a time.

To do anything great is a matter of waking each morning and learning to bless the timetable of God. Patience is that inner peace that comes from agreeing that God, who has all the time in the world, cannot be hurried. Working on God's good time and enjoying God while you labor are the keys to patience.

Questions for Personal Reflection

1. What demands in your life require great patience?

2. How can you reflect God's patience to those with whom you live and work?

Day 7: Group Discussion

The following questions should take about forty-five minutes to answer and discuss. Each member should answer the first question, leaving the remaining questions open-ended. Everyone need not answer, but be sure all members participate.

1. *If you had been in Noah's situation, how would you have responded to God's order that an ark be built? How long would you have worked without questioning or doubting God?*

2. *In what areas of life is it most difficult to be patient?*

3.   *How does anxiety affect the spiritual vibrancy of God's children?*

4.   *What are some ways in which God has rescued you? How can your past experiences serve as an encouragement for you and for others?*

5. How can our past experiences uniquely qualify us for ministry to other believers?

6. How does ego affect one's ability to minister to others? What can we do to control our egos?

Week 2: Patience Brings the Blessing of God

Memory Passage for the Week: Romans 12:11–12

Day 1: Patience Brings the Blessing of God

Praying patiently, especially in times of hardship, means to attune ourselves to God's timetable. 1 Samuel 1:11, 27

Day 2: The Purpose of God in My Life

Christ reminded the church of Philadelphia that patient endurance under trial was the key to God's special protection. Revelation 3:10.

Day 3: My Relationship with Christ

Suffring gilds our hurt with Christlikeness—for Christ himself also suffered unjustly. Therefore, suffering is a direct route to the blessings of God. 1 Peter 2:18–20.

Day 4: My Service to Others

Celebrate all those who act patiently in their service. They have found the fruit of patience. Proverbs 15:18.

Day 5: My Personal Worship

God keeps all his promises, and fulfillment comes to the descendants of those who counted on his integrity and worshiped accordingly. Hebrews 11:39–40.

Day 6: A Character Study on Elisha

2 Kings 2:1–15

Day 7: Group Discussion

Day 1: Patience Brings the Blessing of God
Read 1 Samuel 1:11, 27

Prayers are prayed from our time frame, but they are all answered from God's timetable. So, perhaps the most unreasonable of all intercessions is: "Give this to me now!" Yet this is sometimes how we pray. We don't just ask God for *what* we want, but we tell him *when* we want it. Philippians 4:6 makes it clear that we are to make our petitions to God. Jesus told us that whatever we ask, ask believing, and we shall receive.

Patience in our petitioning marks the stretch between God's answering schedule and our asking schedule. Many of us have known women who have prayed patiently for their husbands to become Christians. Yet their prayers are sometimes not answered for years.

Hannah knew this great truth: praying means we attune ourselves to the timetable of God. No one can speed an answer by trying to push God. "God, answer me *now*" is not a prayer but a case of spiritual nerves. We must always pray, "God, answer me when you will, how you will. I set my watch, even now, by heaven's clock."

The length of time between our requests and God's reply requires patience. Hannah received exactly what she asked for. The key to God's faithfulness lay in her steadfastness. Hannah lived and prayed, worked and prayed, ate and prayed, slept and prayed. She is not to be commended just for being patient with God. She is to be commended for praying without ceasing. Finally, in the longsuffering of her trust, she had a child.

Nothing much changed for Hannah; she kept on praying, praying—ever praying. And you may be sure that Samuel was not the last reply God ever gave to her continuing prayer life. For walking in prayer and waiting in prayer is patience of the highest sort, and it always brings the blessings of God.

Questions for Personal Reflection

1. What are your prayers that have yet to be answered?

2. How can you make prayer a part of your every activity?

Day 2: The Purpose of God in My Life
Read Revelation 3:10

This passage, like the one in 1 Peter, made the point that those who endure hurt with patience are behaving like Christ. Not only is their pain noticed by God but he walks with them through every step of the suffering.

During the 1992 Barcelona Olympics, Derek Redmond popped a hamstring as he ran the 400-meter semifinal race. The tendon's snap was so loud that it sounded like rifle fire to those around the athlete. Young Redmond, who had trained all his life for the event, collapsed in pain on the track. Though he had trained all his life for this big race, he would not place. It looked as though he would not even finish.

But, no!

A tall gentleman made his way down onto the track; he elbowed his way through the crowd and past a security guard to the athlete, who was hobbling his way to the finish line. It was Derek's father. He couldn't help him win, for the race was now over. But he could help him cross the finish line. Redmond steadied himself on his father's strong frame, and together he and his dad limped to the finish line.

Was Redmond disappointed? Of course. Yet of all of the events of that Olympics, the athlete most of us would never forget was Derek Redmond and his father, whose love made it possible for his son to finish the race.

The race we run for the pleasure of Christ is not ours. We are running the course God's love demands. And his accompaniment is sure. The finish line is also not ours. But our Father guarantees us that whatever challenges and difficulties the race demands, we shall not finish it alone.

Patience! The blessing of God is on the way. He may not give you the gold medal in the race of life, but you have his guarantee that you will not have to cross the finish line alone. God is there! Your affliction has meaning. Your pain is understood. The God of the universe aches to see your patient suffering and bombard you with such blessings. Only eternity will bear the weight of your final joy!

Questions for Personal Reflection

1. When have you experienced suffering that turned out to be a positive, or learning experience when it was all said and done?

2. When do you feel most like giving up on your spiritual "race"? How do you get through those hard times?

Day 3: My Relationship with Christ
Read 1 Peter 2:18–20

One cannot read this passage in the book of Peter without being reminded that in Philippians 3:10, Paul promised that we will become spiritually mature by sharing in the fellowship of Christ's sufferings. Peter wrote this passage to help slaves find some meaning in the severity of their abuses. He could not answer all the slaves' questions on the subject, but their pain is a reminder to us that suffering can cause us to focus on God, and that focus will steady us in the painful walk through the valley of our travails.

Pain! How we turn from it. When we are under its muddy gloom, we rarely find the strength to "give thanks in all circumstances" (1 Thessalonians 5:18). Yet beyond the hurt and struggle we realize that had it not been for the pain, we would not have gained a clearer picture of Christ.

Pain is never ours alone. I remember a time when our village doctor had to put some stitches in our little girl's forehead. She had received a deep gash on the front of her face when her very small brother threw his peg board at her. I could not help but notice that as the doctor made his stitches, she fixed her eyes on her mother's eyes, and the interlocking of their gazes made her pain bearable.

This is something like the lesson Peter gave those who had suffered for no good reason. "Fix your eyes on the eyes of God," he essentially said, and while the pain will be there, gazing patiently at your Father in heaven will turn your hurt into a season of blessing in your life. In time you will see it as such a blessing that if you had your whole life to live over again, you would not leave this painful season out. For your suffering will have meaning like that of Christ, who "when he suffered, he made no threats. Instead, he entrusted himself to him who judges justly" (1 Peter 2:23).

Questions for Personal Reflection

1. What have your painful experiences taught you about God's love for you?

2. How can you remain upbeat and positive even in the midst of suffering and pain?

Day 4: My Service to Others

Read Proverbs 15:18

We all want to serve others, but we have to admit that, at times, there is some truth in the sour adage that *hell is other people*. It is so hard to be patient when the kingdom of God seems to be filled with those who have been saved but have done so little growing in the image of Christ. We must be honest: it is sometimes easier to overlook our own immaturity than to overlook the same qualities in someone else. Oh, that we might be as generous to excuse the faults in others that exist within ourselves.

We sing so many songs like, "When we all get to heaven, what a day of rejoicing that will be." But the truth is that we are going to be with a lot of people up there who didn't necessarily bring us much joy down here. It is hard to be patient with those we know. One time after a particularly hard and ugly church business conference, where brothers and sisters were praying through clenched teeth, my son remarked to me, "Dad, will all these people be in heaven?"

"Most of them, son," I allowed.

"Well," he said, "when I get to heaven, I'm going to ask to live by some new people that I don't know so well."

No wonder the book of Proverbs blessed the man and woman who poured the oil of peace and patience on human squabbles. Surely such patience brings the blessings of God.

Questions for Personal Reflection

1. When and where are your most peaceful times?

2. How can you allow God's peace to overcome the natural turmoil of life?

Day 5: My Personal Worship
Read Hebrews 11:38–40

One of the tenderest of all the verses in the Bible is Hebrews 11:38. In mentioning the hideous deaths of the martyrs, this wonderful verse says, "The world was not worthy of them." How true. Martyrs often die young, but they nearly always outperform their killers.

Oddly, most of those who over the years have held the matches that started the fires were church members who believed they were doing God a service by burning people they felt were lesser disciples than they were.

Arrogance lights such heinous fires.

Many a martyr must have died feeling that the God he served was out to lunch at his time of need. Yet in a tender exposé of faithfulness, the writer of Hebrews said, "These were all commended for their faith, yet none of them received what had been promised. God had planned something better for us" (vv. 39–40).

And what is that plan? Who can say for sure? It will not be entirely consummated until Jesus splits the skies, and history is finished. And then we will know the end result of all truth. God never lies. All that he has promised will come to be when we have waited long enough. And in the meantime, we are to praise him, even in the midst of our struggles and our waiting. In the end, patience will at last pour on us glory immeasurable.

Questions for Personal Reflection

1. How does your attitude toward other people affect your relationship with God?

2. What are some things we can do to replace our attitudes with the attitude of God?

Day 6: Elisha—Waiting on God's Timetable
Read 2 Kings 2:1–15

Patience is not passivity. Patience is informed waiting. We wait because we understand that God has an answer, and that we will be at peace, though not completely fulfilled, until that answer comes. Elisha knew what he wanted. He actively waited for what he could not attain by charging the gates of God.

The difference between Elijah and Elisha is the issue of where the waiting is to be done. Elijah said to Elisha: "Stay here; the LORD has sent me to Bethel" (2 Kings 2:2). But Elisha said to Elijah, "As surely as the LORD lives and as you live, I will not leave you" (v. 2). So the two of them went along having this same conversation at Bethel, at Jericho, and at Jordan (vv. 2, 4, 6).

When they crossed the Jordan, Elijah rolled his cloak and struck the waters. The river parted, and they walked across on dry ground. The power of Elijah's mantle amazed the young prophet, but it was not power he was after. He wanted the kind of relationship with God that Elijah had.

On they traveled.

Finally the conversation changed a bit, and Elijah asked Elisha, "'Tell me, what can I do for you before I am taken from you?'

'Let me inherit a double portion of your spirit,' Elisha replied" (v. 9).

"You have asked a difficult thing," Elijah said to Elisha, "yet if you see me when I am taken from you, it will be yours—otherwise not" (v. 10). And so the two of them continued on together until the chariot of fire separated them, and Elijah was whisked away forever. Not only did Elisha see it happen, but Elijah's cloak fluttered down out of heaven and landed at the young prophet's feet. Then Elisha picked up the cloak and walked back to the Jordan. He approached the river and must have wondered, *Can I do what Elijah did?* He struck the river with Elijah's cloak and cried, "Where now is the LORD, the God of Elijah?" (v. 14). The river receded just as it did for Elijah, and Elisha then knew the product of his patience.

Patience achieves our hearts' greatest hunger, but without hurriedness. In Elisha's case, the hunger was for a double portion of Elijah's spirit. He got what he waited for, but his wait was not a yawning, sleepy activity in which God dumped his life goal on him while he snoozed. His waiting was an active patience. He knew how to wait with ardent hope. All who honor such waiting are blessed with the best gifts of God, the final product of all patience.

Elisha demonstrated that patience means pacing the heart. Patience is never a sprinter, and rarely a jogger. Patience is a steady walker. It will not let anxiety rush things along, lest that zeal cause the walker to run—right past God.

Questions for Personal Reflection

1. What amazing things have you seen God do on your behalf or on the behalf of

someone you know?

2. How have those "miracles" affected your walk with God?

Day 7: Group Discussion

The following questions should take about forty-five minutes to answer and discuss. Each member should answer the first question, leaving the remaining questions open-ended. Everyone need not answer, but be sure all members participate.

1.   *Why is it so hard for us to wait for God's answers to our prayers?*

2.   *How can we help each other fix our eyes on God?*

3. *How do you know that God is accompanying you on life's race?*

4. *What does our sensitivity to the faults of others say about our perception of our own faults?*

5. What is the overall effect of a believer's animosity toward other believers? How can we develop God's attitude toward others?

6. What is the hunger of your heart and how is God developing patience in you as you seek to satisfy that hunger?

Week 3: Patience—Victory over Clock & Calendar

Memory Passage for the Week: Psalm 90:12

Day 1: Patience—Victory over Clock and Calendar

The finite timetables of our time on earth should not make us *hurry* our lives, but instead force us to *use* our lives for God's purpose. 2 Kings 20:1–7.

Day 2: The Purpose of God in My Life

No one can outrun the clock and calendar. Still, we may triumph over them by being great stewards of each day, of each moment we have. Job 7:6.

Day 3: My Relationship with Christ

Who by worry can add a single hour to life? Why not give ourselves instead to patience? Christ has saved us; we need not worry. Matthew 6:27.

Day 4: My Service to Others

If we serve only ourselves and achieve money and success, we have really wasted our short time on earth with unfulfilling accomplishments. Luke 12:16–21.

Day 5: My Personal Worship

Patience is a spiritual habit that keeps us paced, even when the threats of life make us anxious. Daniel 6:10.

Day 6: A Character Study on Job

Job 1:1–5, 20–22

Day 7: Group Discussion

Day 1: Patience—Victory over Clock and Calendar
Read 2 Kings 20:1–7

"I'll die when my number's up" is a saying that doesn't take into account the message in Scripture. Hezekiah was a king whose number was up, but he turned his face to the wall and begged God for an extension. God answered and extended Hezekiah's life fifteen more years.

Patience is not begging for enough seconds to help us meet our deadlines. Patience is a paced life that approaches deadlines steadily, confidently, and unhurriedly. Patience is the assumption that every agenda that forces us toward panic should be manually set on "slow down." The journey toward the deadline should hold as much promise as the deadline itself. Hezekiah did not want to die. After all, who wants to die? Most Christians are confident about eternity. We all want to go to heaven when we die. But none of us want to go "on the next load." In spite of the fact that we are counting on heaven being better than this world, we cling to this world as tightly as we can for as long as we can.

Hezekiah, at the hour of death, begged for more life. We can't blame him, for really, when is any life long enough? One can only imagine Methuselah at the gates of death asking God for another nine hundred years, or maybe even ninety more days! Still, Hebrews reminds us that it is appointed unto each of us to die once. Since the last heartbeat is an approaching reality, maybe patience would teach us that the heartbeats along the way are the way we reckon with our finality.

Hezekiah's life was extended. Aren't you curious about how he spent his final fifteen years? Perhaps he lived the paced life. Perhaps he looked at sundials and was determined that they would not master him, but inform him. Perhaps this time around, time would not make him *hurry* life, but it would make him *use* life—all of it—for God's purpose.

Questions for Personal Reflection

1. If you had a limited number of years to live, what would be your top three priorities?

2. How can you make the priorities listed above your priorities for today?

Day 2: The Purpose of God in My Life
Read Job 7:6

Job lamented that his days were swifter than a weaver's shuttle. They were not only brief, they were pointless. Routine is simultaneously our killer and our savior. To get up and do the same thing every day gives us a way to live and a logical reason to get out of bed each morning. But Job's reaction was one often made by people whose routines do not furnish them with meaning. Job had to cry out in his despair, for all the requirements of his life weren't providing him with much hope. Still, Job realized the brevity of life and determined to focus on those values that the passing of time cannot steal.

What were those values? What makes values valuable?

Only one thing: these values were assigned by God. The sense of the hurriedness of life belongs to us all—those who use their time well and those who don't. But those who give their days and years to God do triumph over time. If you want to live with victory, picture yourself taking the clock, laying it on the high altar of God, and asking him to sanctify that clock.

Job, like all of us, still had to get up, even on those hopeless days, and determine to pace his living. Only then could he live with purpose. The habit of patience is reflective. It thinks a lot about God and puts a point to seemingly pointless days.

Patience—the pacing of our affairs—says to the hurried, frantic clocks that surround us: *You can speed my day toward the grave, but I alone determine the quality of meaning those days will hold.*

Questions for Personal Reflection

1. How would you describe the pace of your living?

2. What changes do you need to make in order to slow down the pace of your living?

Day 3: My Relationship with Christ
Read Matthew 6:27

Patience points an instructive finger at our schedule and reprimands our hurried lifestyles, saying, *You cannot force me into running at your pace just to serve your agenda.*

The playwright Henrik Ibsen said that mental illness is always an extreme case of self-absorption. The word *always* may be too strong, for some kinds of mental illness relate to chemical imbalance, and still others result from losses the mentally ill have suffered—losses over which they had little, if any, control.

Still, self-absorption is a real killer of the soul. It causes us to hurry ever faster to avoid the disasters with which it threatens us. Impatience may, in some cases, be our attempt at self-preservation. We believe that if we hurry, we will avoid some dire circumstances that threaten our self-esteem. Impatience, therefore, becomes a kind of self-absorption. It masquerades as seriousness about life. Patience then seems to be a sign we are blasé about success. It becomes a kind of self-threat. Those who will not hurry seem to us to be lazy. They seem to be in grave danger of becoming irrelevant as a result of not taking life seriously. Such impatience does less harm in the end than the pace it dictates.

Jesus said the mental frenzy that we hope will give us one more inch of height is to no avail. Since such inner turmoil is pointless, why not give ourselves instead to patience? Christ has saved us. We need not worry about the future.

Patience walks slow and shouts to that self-absorption that would cause us to hurry. To succeed is not to hurry toward success. It is to trust God, walk slowly, and see the world we once overlooked in the rush.

Questions for Personal Reflection

1. Is it more normal for you to be in a hurry or to move at a more deliberate pace? What are the positives and negatives associated with each speed?

2. How does your patience (or lack of patience) affect your relationships with other people?

Day 4: My Service to Others

Read Luke 12:16–21

Greed is an impetus to hurry faster. The rich man in the parable in Luke 12:16–21 fell for the common notion that he would be richer if he just pushed harder. So the rich man built bigger barns to certify his future. We are spared many of the details of his barn building, but he seems to be the kind of man who set deadlines for the builders. No doubt he fidgeted when he saw all that he had to get done, always finishing later than he would have liked. Getting rich required running. And running consumed his life.

William Wordsworth, in his famous and wonderful sonnet "Composed Upon Westminster Bridge", causes us to recall that "late or soon, getting and spending, we lay waste our powers."[1] What the rich man did not stop to ask was: "What might I be doing if I were not forever building barns? To what more meaningful activities might I devote my life?"

Greed inspires the current generation of barn builders. Patience is not the mode of Wall Street. Buy now! Eat fast food! Don't wait on anything! To this hassled generation God whispers: *Slow down. See the needy world and serve it.* To serve only yourself is to die before the day your barn constructions are finished. You can only beat the clock by refusing to race it.

Questions for Personal Reflection

1. How does greed affect your life?

2. Greed sometimes is a by-product of competitive living. Against whom are you competing and why?

Day 5: My Personal Worship
Read Daniel 6:10

Daniel prayed in his crisis "just as he had done before" (Daniel 6:10). It is safe to say that Daniel was pacing his life with prayer. Those who believe in the importance of prayer do a rather remarkable thing in this hurried, overscheduled world of ours. They simply stop running and take perfectly good time they could use for success and achievement to pray. Why? Because to pray is to succeed. To arrive at any plateau of personal advancement having not prayed is to get there the wrong way.

Prayer changes things, but the most important thing it changes is *us*. This is perhaps the first thing we should see about prayer and the last thing we usually do see. So many intercessors spend their time asking God for changes they want to see in the world and, while seeing some of it, fail to see that the biggest and best changes happened in them personally.

Prayer keeps us flexible and willing to modify or erase those personal parts of our ambitions that make us most neurotic. Notice the methodology of Daniel's prayer routine:

1. He left what he had been doing.
2. He went home where he could be alone with God.
3. He climbed the stairs to his quiet altar.
4. He opened the windows toward Jerusalem.

5. He knelt down to pray.

6. He repeated this routine three times a day.

It is easy to see that Daniel had a prayer routine that broke into the demands of all his other routines. It was his prayer routine that gave his hassled business routine a purpose.

Questions for Personal Reflection

1. Are your prayers more concerned with getting something from God or communicating with him?

2. What are some of the things that prevent you from praying as you should?

Day 6: Job—Enduring Meaningful Suffering

Read Job 1:1–5, 20–22

Patience is how the godly mind occupies itself when it can't find a decent answer to the question, *Why do the righteous suffer?* Therefore, patience is the art of innocent suffering. Patience means loving God even when he is silent. Patience means crediting God with knowing what's best, even when troubles come upon us in battalions, clouding our horizons of hope.

Job was the godliest of men. He was blameless and upright. He feared God and shunned evil. He never forgot the spiritual needs of his family. Early every morning he would sacrifice a burnt offering for each of his children just in case they had committed any sin that day (Job 1:2, 5). Because Job was extremely wealthy, everyone assumed that God was simply honoring his righteousness (v. 3). But then, in a remarkably short period of time, all of Job's children and their families were tragically killed, and all his wealth was gone. "At this, Job got up and tore his robe and shaved his head.... In all this, Job did not sin by charging God with wrongdoing" (vv. 20, 22).

How did Job react to his suffering?

First, he complained of his suffering (but then doesn't everybody): "If only my anguish could be weighed and all my misery be placed on the scales! It would surely outweigh the sand of the seas" (Job 6:2–3).

Second, he philosophized over his lot in life: "Does not man have hard service on earth? Are not his days like those of a hired man? ... I loathe my very life; therefore I will give free rein to my complaint.... Man born of woman is of few days and full of trouble" (Job 7:1; 10:1; 14:1).

Finally, he wished he had never been born at all, saying, "May the day of my birth perish, and the night it was said, 'A boy is born!'" (Job 3:3).

When we don't fully understand the reason we're on the planet, it is of great comfort to read Job's benedictions over what seemed to him his own pointless life. Suffering is never meaningless—of that we can be certain. And in reading of Job's endurance through extreme suffering, we know we can hold on yet a while:

> *Naked I came from my mother's womb,*
> *and naked I will depart.*
> *The LORD gave and the LORD has taken away;*
> *may the name of the LORD be praised.*
> —Job 1:21

Suffering hurts so badly that sometimes the only balm that can heal it is praise. It is those who cry who sing the sweetest songs to God. Such songs are never hurried. They are born in patience and sung in soft acceptance.

Questions for Personal Reflection

1. When you suffer, what is your initial cry to God?

2. How long does it take for you to realize the value of your suffering? Why does it take this long?

Day 7: Group Discussion

The following questions should take about forty-five minutes to answer and discuss. Each member should answer the first question, leaving the remaining questions open-ended. Everyone need not answer, but be sure all members participate.

1. *What valuable lessons have resulted from times you have suffered?*

2. *What are the grand plans for which you are living? Are they yours or are they God's?*

3. *Why do we live such frantic lives? What can we do to slow down?*

4. *Why is patience sometimes viewed as laziness? What is the difference between being lazy and being patient?*

5.   *How are we affected by our society's bent toward greed?*

6.   *If prayer paces life, then at what pace are we living? Why are we often too hurried to pray?*

Week 4: Patience—The Unhurried Virtue

Memory Passage for the Week: Exodus 14:13–14

Day 1: Patience—The Unhurried Virtue

Forgiveness requires patience. God is patient with us and forgives our sins, just as we need patience in order to forgive others. Matthew 18:21–35.

Day 2: The Purpose of God in My Life

Patience is the virtue that demonstrates that we are fully in touch and at ease with the purposes of God in our lives. Deuteronomy 34:5–8.

Day 3: My Relationship with Christ

Patience is a virtue that is born by not assuming that we have all the time we would like to accomplish all the goals we would like. Psalm 39:1–4.

Day 4: My Service to Others

The world's salvation is not an *en masse* event. God is patient, knowing it will occur as people come into the kingdom one confession at a time. Matthew 10:32–34.

Day 5: My Personal Worship

When Nehemiah read the Word of God all day long, the Word was all transforming. And the listeners were riveted to its glory. Nehemiah 8:9–10.

Day 6: A Character Study on Mary

Luke 1:26–38

Day 7: Group Discussion

Day 1: Patience—The Unhurried Virtue

Read Matthew 18:21–35

The issue of patience was occasioned by Peter's asking, "How many times shall I forgive my brother when he sins against me? Up to seven times?" (Matthew 18:21). Peter felt magnanimous in suggesting sevenfold forgiveness as some kind of worldwide standard. But Jesus reminded him that a better standard would be seventy times seven, or roughly 490 times. Jesus was not advancing some legalistic rule here. The idea was that when you reached 243 times or so, you would probably just quit counting and maybe become more willing, like God, to forgive freely and without a credit and debit calculator system.

Here's how Jesus' parable would look in today's world. Someone named Sue offends someone named Bill. Sue says, "I'm sorry, Bill, will you forgive me?"

"Certainly, Sue. It was nothing, forget it," says Bill.

Then Sue sins the same sin again.

"I'm sorry, Bill, will you forgive me?"

"Certainly, Sue, but try not to do it again."

Then Sue sins the same sin again.

"I'm sorry, Bill, will you forgive me?"

"Well ... okay, but this has got to stop, okay?"

Then Sue sins the same sin again.

"I'm sorry, Bill, will you forgive me?"

"Well ... let me think about it and I'll get back to you."

Patience is an unhurried virtue. Patience waits and forgives, and waits and forgives. Meanwhile Bill, who wishes Sue would get a hold on her moral inconsistencies, also sins. It's the same sin he always sins against God, and he goes in before the Lord and says, "Oh, God, I know I've begged your forgiveness a thousand times for this same sin, but will you forgive me just this once more?"

And Bill is surprised to hear God's answer: "I don't know, Bill, did you ever get back to Sue?"

Questions for Personal Reflection

1. When you ask God to forgive you, he does. Why can't we forgive ourselves?

2. How can your time alone with God help you maintain moral consistency?

Day 2: The Purpose of God in My Life
Read Deuteronomy 34:5–8

The life of Moses seems to have been divisible by three. His total 120-year life span was a triad of three forty-year segments, during the first of which he was involved as official royalty in Egypt. The second forty years he spent in the wilderness of Sinai, and then at eighty years of age or so he traveled back to Egypt, arranged for the Exodus, and led the people in and around Sinai for the last forty years of his life.

But there is a wistful something about this passage in Deuteronomy 34:5–8. Vital for all his years, Moses did not enter Canaan. The years must have come flooding over him all at once, and his reckoning with them was probably a study in steely patience.

Deuteronomy is composed mainly of the last three farewell addresses that Moses made to Israel. But tacked on to the end of these sermons is one short chapter describing Moses' rugged state of health and his death and burial on Mount Nebo. For all his greatness, nobody knows to this day where his grave is (Deuteronomy 34:6).

I like thinking that Moses lived a well-paced life, and that his struggle with patience was a battle that he, like all of us, sometimes won and sometimes lost. Because he lacked patience at the rock, he was condemned to never enter Canaan. But the presence of his patience so many other times in his journeys with the nation of Israel must have been the reason that he lived so long and led so well.

At the end of Moses' final sermon, he read one of his poems to the Israelites. It stands as a celebration of his patience—the unhurried virtue—and also as an epitaph for his life:

> *Remember the days of old;*
> *consider the generations long past.*
> *Ask your father and he will tell you;*
> *your elders, and they will explain to you.*
> *When the Most High gave the nations their inheritance,*
> *when he divided all mankind,*
> *he set up boundaries for the peoples*
> *according to the number of the sons of Israel.*
> —Deuteronomy 32:7–8

Questions for Personal Reflection

1. When has a lack of patience gotten you into trouble? What has patience saved you from getting into trouble or making a wrong decision?

2. If your life was divided into three sections, what would be the heading over each section?

Day 3: My Relationship with Christ
Read Psalm 39:1—4

"Show me, O LORD, my life's end and the number of my days; let me know how fleeting is my life" (Psalm 39:4), declared the psalmist.

How fast the days of our lives pass, and if ever we become good stewards, we must find a way to measure the years so they do not steal our sense of patience, but rather improve the stewardship of our lives.

Think of it this way, if you live to be seventy-two years of age and could reckon all the years of your life on one giant clock, you might sequence your life in this manner. Plot all seventy-two years of your intended life span on that twelve-hour dial. Each hour on that dial will then represent six years of your life. You would then be born at seven o'clock in the morning and would die at seven o'clock in the evening. This would mean that when it is eight o'clock on that great life-clock, you are six years old. When it is nine o'clock on that great clock, you are twelve years old.

When it is ten o'clock on that great clock, you are already eighteen years old.

When it is twelve o'clock on that great clock, you are now thirty years old.

When it is four o'clock on that great clock, you are fifty-four years old.

When it is six o'clock you are sixty-six years old and you must die at seven o'clock in the evening.

Indeed the psalmist was right when he wrote, "You have made my days a mere handbreath; the span of my years is as nothing before you. Each man's life is but a breath" (v. 5). Against the fast tumbling years, let us bring a determined patience that these years will all be used for Christ.

Questions for Personal Reflection

1. Do you find yourself thinking more about the past or the future? Why?

2. How can you live in the moment while still planning for the future?

Day 4: My Service to Others
Read Matthew 10:32–34

Confession is the glorious calling of the church. It is the church's great ministry of compassion, for it allows those perishing beyond God's love an eternity of grace.

Confession is a ministry of identity, for it allows men and women to identify with the church by openly naming Jesus as their Lord. Confession furnishes the joy of worship as people in the congregation openly talk about the central love affair of their lives.

There is urgency in our confession, for if people do not find Christ they will perish, and eternity for the unconfessed is uncertain. But there is also to be a well-paced message that takes the time to explain the gospel to the unsaved. We must advance steadily into the world, taking time to thoroughly teach and preach the Good News.

Jesus said in Matthew 10:34 that this will, in some sense, be the most nerve-racking of our work. Why? Because the very word *Jesus,* whose confession brings glory to the church, is at the same time a word that is not welcomed everywhere. Some families have been divided right down the middle over who Jesus is and what his rightful place is in their lives. Some confessions bring applause, and some martyrdom.

But patience, patience, patience. Let the unhurried virtue of steady advance preach the grand truth to all who will receive it. And may we who preach the confessional life be patient, always ready to be kind to those who will not receive the truth, treating them as Christ himself would treat them.

Questions for Personal Reflection

1. Is your life a good advertisement for the Christian life? Why or why not?

2. How can we make our lives more effective advertisements for a life of faith?

Day 5: My Personal Worship
Read Nehemiah 8:9–10

Let us approach worship in an unhurried fashion. Notice in Nehemiah 8:9–10 that Ezra the scribe read the Bible from daybreak till noon, and as far as we can tell from the Hebrew text, no one stood and complained, "Why is this worship service going on so long?"

Worship is a well-paced and unhurried art, and apparently in Israel they knew they had plenty time for it. No one was anxious. They were steady and took all the time they needed for praising God. The worship was mostly given to the reading of the Word of God, although from time to time "all the people lifted their hands and responded, 'Amen! Amen!' Then they bowed down and worshiped the LORD with their faces to the ground" (Nehemiah 8:6).

And how did the Israelites treat the reading of the Word of God? "They read from the Book of the Law of God, making it clear and giving the meaning so that the people could understand what was being read" (v. 8).

But what was the overall response to this long, "your roast back home is probably burning" service? The people wept at the privilege and responsibility and burden of hearing the Word of God spoken directly to them. They broke into weeping before the Word.

It was then that Nehemiah reminded them that the Word sometimes brings us to tears and conviction, but on this particular occasion the Word of God was to be the joy at the center of their party. They had time; the steady virtue called patience was at their side. Nehemiah called out to all the people: "This day is sacred to the LORD, your God. Do not mourn or weep.... Go and enjoy choice food and sweet drinks ... Do not grieve, for the joy of the LORD is your strength" (vv. 9–10).

God is likely to invade our unhurried worship, and we are to take all the time we need, practicing patience during our worship, the steady heart of our praise.

Questions for Personal Reflection

1. What is worship?

2. Is worship for you an attitude of life or something you attend? Explain.

Day 6: Mary—The "Yes-Lord" Mystique

Luke 1:26–38

Patience never argues with God. Back-talk is a primary indicator of impatience. The angel Gabriel assuaged Mary's fear in Luke 1:30, but he did not accuse her of impatience. This passage is a testimony to Mary's steady and obedient walk of patience. Gabriel, after all, did lay on her some pretty heavy news.

First of all, he told her she was going to have a baby when she didn't even have a husband. He also told her that her baby would be both the Messiah and the Son of God. He then told her that this child would be conceived supernaturally by the Holy Spirit—a story that was a hard sell in Nazareth. And so the greatest story ever told began as the hardest story that anyone might ever have had to tell.

The breaking of this big news was answered by Mary's very simple response of obedience, "May it be to me as you have said" (v. 38). It almost makes us want to ask, "Are you sure, Mary? All of it? Can you handle the blitz of gossip over your pregnancy? Can you handle the smirks of quiet disdain when you try to tell others that the child you carry was conceived by the Holy Spirit?"

But Mary had a patient reply for all who would question her for not questioning God: "May it be to me as [God has] said."

Mary was an example of patience, and patience is steady. Patience simply says, *Be it to me even as you have said.* It even has a habit of praising

God while it waits, and so Mary sang:

> *My soul glorifies the Lord*
> *and my spirit rejoices in God my Savior,*
> *for he has been mindful*
> *of the humble state of his servant.*
> *From now on all generations will call me blessed,*
> *for the Mighty One has done great things for me—*
> *holy is his name.*
>
> —Luke 1:46–49

Questions for Personal Reflection

1. Why is it so hard to be patient with God?

2. In what ways do you need to become more patient with him?

Day 7: Group Discussion

The following questions should take about forty-five minutes to answer and discuss. Each member should answer the first question, leaving the remaining questions open-ended. Everyone need not answer, but be sure all members participate.

1. *Why are so many people who know Christians reluctant to become Christians?*

2. *Why is it so easy to accept forgiveness but so hard to give it?*

3. *How might other people perceive your patience as it relates to your ambition and motivation for doing what you do?*

4. *How can we balance planning for the future with the guarantee of nothing beyond the present moment?*

5. *How can we make worship a way of life?*

6. *Why do we so often delay being obedient to God?*

Week 5: Patience—The Slowly Acquired Virtue

Memory Passage for the Week: Psalm 37:7

Day 1: Patience—The Slowly Acquired Virtue

Unfailing patience is not a flaw in God; it is evidence of the glory of God. Nehemiah 9:29–31.

Day 2: The Purpose of God in My Life

God, unhurried for his years, reminds us that he is never through with us. He always has a plan and a purpose for us, even in old age. Luke 1:5–7, 13.

Day 3: My Relationship with Christ

What is glorious about drawing close to Christ is that the closer we draw to perfection, the more our imperfections are apparent to us. 1 Timothy 1:15–16.

Day 4: My Service to Others

In serving others, it is important that both the leaders and the led wait in patience on the specific direction of God. Judges 5:1–2.

Day 5: My Personal Worship

Our worship can be full of the anticipation of God's long-awaited answer to our patient prayers. Romans 8:18–25.

Day 6: The Parable of the Unforgiving Steward

Matthew 18:21–34 (TLB)

Day 7: Group Discussion

Day 1: Patience—The Slowly Acquired Virtue
Read Nehemiah 9:29–31

Historically, God's motif has been patience. God was patient with Israel time and time again, including in Nehemiah 9:29, when:

- 🐛 They became arrogant.
- 🐛 They disobeyed his commandments.
- 🐛 They sinned against God's ordinances.
- 🐛 They turned their backs on his desires for them.
- 🐛 They became stiff-necked and refused to listen.

All of these transgressions brought the judgment of God, and yet Israel still would not listen. But through all of this, God patiently waited on Israel to return his love and behave like his chosen children.

The spirit of this Nehemiah passage is echoed in 2 Peter 3:8–9. Peter said that to our frenzied, earthbound view, God may appear slow in keeping his second-coming promises. But that is not so. God is not slow; he just works off a different timetable than we do. He is deliberate in extending the day when Jesus comes again so that as many as possible may be saved.

"But do not forget this one thing, dear friends: With the Lord a day is like a thousand years and a thousand years are like a day. The Lord is not slow in keeping his promise, as some understand slowness. He is patient with you, not wanting anyone to perish, but for everyone to come to repentance" (2 Peter 3:8–9).

Patience is not a flaw in God; it is evidence of the glory of God. If God can extend his all-important worldwide agenda by pacing himself to save all, perhaps we can do the same.

Questions for Personal Reflection

1. How have you experienced God's patience?

2. How should the second coming of Christ affect the way we interact with other people?

Day 2: The Purpose of God in My Life
Read Luke 1:5–7, 13

For those believers hungry to know and serve God, there is one virtue that is more important than any other: patience. Oh how we wish God would hurry his agenda. How we wish he would give us one little peek into that future that is ever so slow in coming. If we could but pry the calendar from his hand and rip that big watch off his divine wrist. Why are there no clues for tomorrow? Why, when we are so ready to go, is God so late in keeping his appointment with us again this week? God, give us patience, *right now!*

Zechariah and Elizabeth had waited a lifetime, and not until they reached the place where pregnancy was nearly impossible did God finally show up. It is easy to imagine that if it were up to them, they would have preferred that the baby come a bit earlier. But God had a plan and a purpose at work. Of course, God's perfect plan is so much easier to see in hindsight.

God has a plan for our lives. We all enjoy God's plan and agree that once it is being lived out, it is just right for us. But it can take years for God's plan to be made evident to us, and sometimes—on the front side of all that we wait for—we wish that God would move a little faster. But on the back side of the will of God, even Elizabeth and Zechariah would have to agree: not only is the plan right, but it is well worth our patience.

Questions for Personal Reflection

1. How is God gradually revealing his plan for your life?

2. If God revealed his entire plan for your life, would you be excited or scared?

Why?

Day 3: My Relationship with Christ

Read 1 Timothy 1:15–16

How do we view ourselves through the eyes of Christ? Grace is the anti-
dote for our sinfulness. Grace takes into account the darkness of our sins
and washes us clean. Even grace is patient. Paul was, in his own eyes, the
chief of sinners—but then, Christ is the chief of grace. Grace comes to
us as it will, at God's speed; it may seem slow to us, yet always in time to
include us in the beloved.

Would you with Paul say, "I am the chief of sinners"? Yes? Then all
is well, for grace is coming to you; be as patient in your waiting for it as
God is in his coming to you. Author John Bunyan once wrote:

> *O Son of God, grace was in all thy tears; grace came bub-
> bling out of thy side with thy blood; grace came forth with
> every word of thy sweet mouth; grace came out where the
> whip smote thee, where the thorns pricked thee, where the nails
> and spears pierced thee. O Blessed Son of God, here is grace
> indeed! Unsearchable riches of grace! Unthought-of riches of
> grace! Grace to make angels wonder, grace to make sinners
> happy, grace to astonish devils.* [2]

It is with abundant patience that Christ's grace is bestowed upon each
of us. Because we are, as humans and sinners, incapable of such uncondi-

tional patience, it can be difficult to fathom or even accept this amazing love. When we learn to rest in the assurance of Christ's limitless grace and patience with us, we inevitably become more patient with ourselves, with those we love, and even—and perhaps most importantly—with those who sin against us.

The crux of God's patient grace appears in 1 Timothy 1:16: "But for that very reason I was shown mercy so that in me, the worst of sinners, Christ Jesus might display his unlimited patience as an example for those who would believe on him and receive eternal life."

Questions for Personal Reflection

1. What is more powerful in your life—your sinfulness or God's grace?

2. How can you reflect more of God's grace to people who do not know him?

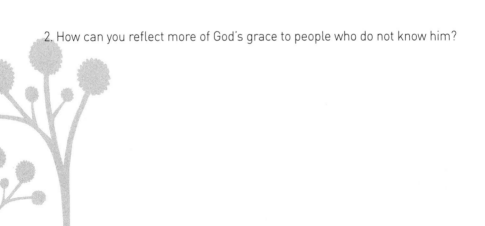

Day 4: My Service to Others
Read Judges 5:1–2

Deborah and Barak sang a long anthem to the victory over their enemies, but the first words of their song reflect the joy that emanates from seeing a whole nation wait on God.

> *When the princes in Israel take the lead,*
> *When the people willingly offer themselves—*
> *Praise the LORD!*
> —Judges 5:2

The leadership in Israel was dependent on inter-cooperative patience. In Deborah's time as a judge, the Israelites came to her to have their disputes decided (Judges 4:5). Deborah sent for Barak to lead Israel in a campaign against their enemy, Sisera. Barak said, "If you go with me, I will go; but if you don't go with me, I won't go" (v. 8).

So it was agreed upon, and together they went. The real hero of the Sisera campaign, however, turned out to be Jael, the wife of Heber the Kenite. She befriended the fleeing and fatigued Sisera, and as he rested in her tent, she drove a tent peg through his head.

Jael is not a major player in the Old Testament, but she stole Barak's thunder just as Deborah had prophesied she would. God's historical pageants have major and minor players, and they only come to pass when everybody works together, patiently trusts God's plan, and takes seriously their role in his perfect plan.

The details of this victorious campaign once again are the result of a group patience that operated between so many in Israel. So Deborah's song was right. When princes lead, and the people offer themselves, and all of them wait on God, victory and blessing proceed. The key is that the leaders and the led must wait in patience on the specific direction of God.

Questions for Personal Reflection

1. In what areas of life are you awaiting God's instructions? How do you expect him to deliver those instructions?

2. In what ways in the past have you been surprised by God's instructions?

Day 5: My Personal Worship

Read Romans 8:18–25

Patience is the grand interpreter of so many unfathomable events in our lives. What are unfathomable events? Romans 8:18–25 is filled with an unusual amount of them.

Here are three events over which each of us must wrestle, usually without any satisfactory explanation:

1. Our present sufferings sometimes afflict us with such pain that we have no idea why God is permitting these things to happen to us (v. 18). Paul offers no real answer except to say that they are not worthy to be compared with the glory that shall be.

2. There is bondage in creation's decay (v. 21). Why does the world die around us? If even the apostle Paul asked this question, how much more will we be justified to ask it? We watch whole species die year after year, and we wonder why there is senseless corruption in creation. In our case, humankind itself seems responsible. Paul says that we are to await the Redeemer's resolution to the problem.

3. Finally, we ourselves are groaning as we wait for God to resolve the very redemption of our bodies (v. 23). Like the creation itself, we are eager for God to finish us up and bring us

to completion in himself. Paul understood that it is patience, but a groaning kind of patience, and we find it hard to wait.

Yet this impatient patience forms a kind of delicious agony at the center of our worship. We wait and groan, but we wait; and as we wait, we anticipate. The anticipation is our response of joy to the certain hope that God has given us: "But if we hope for what we do not have, we wait for it patiently" (v. 25).

Questions for Personal Reflection

1. What unfathomable events have you experienced? How did they affect your relationship with God?

2. In what ways are you living with the patient hope that accompanies faith in God? How can you share that hope with others?

Day 6: The Parable of the Unforgiving Steward

MATTHEW 18:21–34 (TLB)

Then Peter came to [Jesus] and asked, "Sir, how often should I forgive a brother who sins against me? Seven times?"

"No!" Jesus replied, "seventy times seven!"

"The Kingdom of heaven can be compared to a king who decided to bring his accounts up to date. In the process one of his debtors was brought in who owed him $10,000,000! He couldn't pay, so the king ordered him sold for the debt, also his wife and children and everything he had.

"But the man fell down before the king, his face in the dust, and said, 'Oh, sir, be patient with me and I will pay it all.'

"Then the king was filled with pity for him and released him and forgave his debt.

"But when the man left the king, he went to a man who owed him $2,000 and grabbed him by the throat and demanded instant payment.

"The man fell down before him and begged him to give him a little time. 'Be patient and I will pay it,' he pled.

"But the creditor wouldn't wait. He had the man arrested and jailed until the debt would be paid in full.

"Then the man's friends went to the king and told him what had happened. And the king called before him the man he had forgiven and said, 'You evil-hearted wretch! Here I forgave you all that tremendous debt, just because you asked me to—shouldn't you have mercy on others, just as I had mercy on you?'

"Then the angry king sent the man to the torture chamber until he had paid every last penny due. So shall my heavenly Father do to you if you refuse to truly forgive your brothers."

Questions for Personal Reflection

1. God's mercy is ever evident in our lives. What are some ways that you see his mercy in your life?

2. What happens to your spiritual life when you refuse to grant forgiveness to others?

Day 7: Group Discussion

The following questions should take about forty-five minutes to answer and discuss. Each member should answer the first question, leaving the remaining questions open-ended. Everyone need not answer, but be sure all members participate.

1. *What are the lifelong dreams for which you wait?*

2. *In what ways do we need to be more patient with others?*

3. *Why do many believers spend more time condemning sin than dispensing God's grace? Which do you do?*

4. *Why do we make our decisions, live with the consequences, and then seek God's direction? What would happen if we reversed the process?*

5. *How do we explain God's miracles to people who do not know him?*

6. *How have we been the beneficiaries of God's mercy? How can we reflect that mercy to others?*

Week 6: Patience—Waiting for God's Promises

Memory Passage for the Week: 1 Peter 5:10

Day 1: Patience—Waiting for God's Promises

God has many things to show us when the time is right. Until then the wait itself is wonderful. Luke 2:25–32.

Day 2: The Purpose of God in My Life

If we learn how to trust and wait, said the prophet Isaiah, we shall float above the hassled world and see it as God does. Isaiah 40:31.

Day 3: My Relationship with Christ

Waiting with Christ is indeed a pleasant way to approach what we know will be even more pleasant. 1 John 3:2.

Day 4: My Service to Others

To be in the service of God is to serve in such a way that we wait, take responsibility, and, no matter how menial our duties, thank him for the privilege to serve. Numbers 4:21–28.

Day 5: My Personal Worship

When we wait on God, we can do so with a joyful heart, for we know our prayers will be answered. We can worship while we wait. Genesis 13:1–4.

Day 6: Verses for Further Reflection

Day 7: Group Discussion

Day 1: Patience—Waiting for God's Promises
Read Luke 2:25–32

Old Simeon had waited all his life for a glimpse of the Messiah. Then in the endless line of those who came to offer worship at the temple, the old man saw at last the baby he had waited all his life to see. It is not often that old men are granted the longed-for fulfillment to all their dreams. But Simeon was granted this fulfillment, and he praised God, saying: "Sovereign Lord, as you have promised, you now dismiss your servant in peace" (Luke 2:29).

It is a wonderful thing to die an old man who measured every promise of God and found not a single one of them wanting. So God put the leathery old face of a patriarch next to the fresh new skin of a baby. And the contrast between an old, wrinkled visage and a new child is the picture of how God furnishes every new generation with hope. But in Simeon's case, it was more than that—it was confirmation that God always keeps his promises. The old man is proof that God can be depended upon for a lifetime. God always keeps his promises. But the baby shows that God will save, and that is what put the sparkle in the old man's eye.

The infant Christ shows that God is going to change the heart of humankind, and when the change is through, eternity and time will be indistinguishable.

"My eyes have seen your salvation" (v. 30).

In this statement is the realized product of patience. God has many things to show us when the time is right. Until then the wait itself is wonderful.

Questions for Personal Reflection

1. For what are you waiting? How can you convert your wait into faithful hope?

2. What are you depending on God for today? Tomorrow? Next year? Ten years from now?

Day 2: The Purpose of God in My Life
Read Isaiah 40:31

Those who wait on the Lord, who walk with him in patience, demonstrate the power of true inner spirituality. Here then is the fourfold virtue
of godly patience. In Isaiah 40:31, we are reassured that those who wait
upon the Lord:

1. *Will renew their strength.* Here is the physical testament of a spiritual truth. Is it possible that God can make strong our ebbing
   physical strength, just by our asking? It is indeed possible.
2. *Will mount up with wings as eagles.* Spiritual elation is another result
   of waiting on God. Have you not experienced the buoyancy
   at the end of a long period of spiritual waiting? You wait and
   pray and pray and wait, and then a wonderful breakthrough
   comes. Jesus invades our hearts, and all things ponderous and
   plodding finally grow wings. Suddenly we soar in faith, and
   heaven is nearer than we supposed it might be.
3. *Will run and not be weary.* Waiting on God supplies an energy
   for life we may have never known we had. Take, for example,
   an older missionary doctor who was forced by age to return
   home. When asked if he was glad for the rest, he said yes.
   "But," he went on, "when my clinic was full, and people were
   walking for miles to stand in line for treatment—when I never

got a day off, and I worked till midnight treating their bodies and winning their souls ... oh, those were the days!" There is a grand inebriation in serving God by doing something we really believe in. We run and are never weary.

4. *Will walk and not faint.* Running is not the way to demonstrate steadiness. All who run must sometimes stop to walk. But those who walk can walk forever ... steadily ... well-paced and patiently free in Christ.

Patience brings it all: the renewed strength, the soaring elation, and the marathon running that is glorious in its intent.

Questions for Personal Reflection

1. How would embracing your purpose in life improve your desire to walk and not faint?

2. What are some insignificant things that you might be able to eliminate in order to slow down the pace of your life?

Day 3: My Relationship with Christ
Read 1 John 3:2

We who daily follow Christ await the finished picture of ourselves. We shall be like him, and we shall appear as he appears. It is enough to make our waiting glorious and our patience well rewarded.

The French theologian François Fénelon said long ago that patience itself works hand in hand with love, and love makes everything easy.

> *Jesus Christ said to all Christians without exception, "Let him who would be my disciple carry his cross, and follow me." The broad way leads to perdition. We must follow the narrow way which few enter. We must be born again, renounce ourselves, hate ourselves, become a child, be poor in spirit, weep to be comforted, and not be of the world which is cursed because of its scandals.*
>
> *These truths frighten many people, and this is because they only know what religion exacts without knowing what it offers, and they ignore the spirit of love which makes everything easy. They do not know that it leads to the highest perfection by a feeling of peace and love which sweetens all the struggle.*[3]

So patience causes us to trust God's love and wait. The wait discovers his promises by majoring on our relationship with Christ.

Questions for Personal Reflection

1. When we focus on our relationships with others, we grow impatient. When we focus on our relationship with God, we become more patient. Based on your patience, on what are you more focused?

2. Patience while on this earth produces a life that points others to God. Is your life pointing others to him? Why or why not?

Day 4: My Service to Others
Read Numbers 4:21–28

The Gershonites were servants in their time. They served Israel in a humble way, and yet their service was far from lowly. You see, the Gershonites were responsible for packing and transporting the canvas and the hangings of that portable cathedral called the tabernacle.

The Gershonites seemed to have accepted God's lot in life for them. And so they packed and transported. I've often wondered if someday, in an old clay jar sealed for 3,500 years, there might be found a papyrus tablet—a testimony of one of the lost Gershonites which might read:

> *I am a Gershonite,*
> *There's no use wishing I was a Levite.*
> *The Levites get to wear the fine vestments, the golden ephods*
> *And things like that.*
> *We Gershonites but carried the tabernacle, a thousand, hot-sand miles,*
> *Through the Sinai wilderness.*
> *It was not a job that made for glory or historical remembrance.*
> *But it was a job by which God daily measured our patience.*
> *And when we'd folded and unfolded the tabernacle of our God, for the*
> *thousandth time*
> *We rejoiced!*
> *Our service made it possible for Israel to worship.*

And if they have forgotten us,

It matters not, for God never forgets.

Especially does he love those who serve in patience.

He blesses those at every sunset

for all they've done that will never be remembered.

The spirit of the Gershonites must be ours. God calls us out of grumbling servitude to patient joy. Let us do his will. Let us not ask why God does not call us to a more glamorous job, but why he called us as worthy to serve him at any job. Come then, let us rejoice. God has called us. Patient obedience is our promised reward.

Questions for Personal Reflection

1. How can God use you right now where you are?

2. How can today's experiences prepare you for tomorrow's uncertainties?

Day 5: My Personal Worship

Read Genesis 13:1–3

The wait is the relationship. The wait is the remembrance. Abraham built an altar at Bethel. He actually rebuilt it and returned to the place where he had first entered Canaan and took his first baby steps in trust. There he first met with God in following his covenant course of patience. There he renewed it all over again for the future.

Abraham must have meditated at Bethel the whys and wherefores of covenant faith. God had called him, and he followed in patience. But at every altar, he must have thought, *Why? Why me, God? Why of all people in the world should I be so central to your saving dreams for all humankind?*

Joseph Bayley, the wonderful evangelical thinker, wrote of the wonderment of the call:

> *King Jesus*
> *why did you choose me*
> *a lowly unimportant person*
> *to bear you*
> *in my world today?*
> *I'm poor and unimportant*
> *trained to work*
> *not carry kings*
> *—let alone the King of kings*

and yet you've chosen me
to carry you in triumph
in this world's parade.[4]

When we wait on God, we can do so with a joyful heart, for we know our prayers will be answered. We know God's promises will be fulfilled. There is joy in the waiting. There is worship in our patience.

Questions for Personal Reflection

1. Is waiting on God something you enjoy? Why or why not?

2. How can your waiting on God become an educational experience for those around you?

Day 6: Verses for Further Reflection

Romans 12:12: Be joyful in hope, patient in affliction.

Ephesians 4:2: Be completely humble and gentle; be patient, bearing with one another in love.

Colossians 1:11: Being strengthened with all power according to his glorious might so that you may have great endurance and patience.

1 Thessalonians 5:14: And we urge you, brothers, warn those who are idle, encourage the timid, help the weak, be patient with everyone.

2 CORINTHIANS 11:16–33

Paul was patient with his God so that he would not move presumptuously into any area of ministry. In this passage he enumerated his suffering and explained that the outcome of all of the suffering was patience.

I repeat: Let no one take me for a fool. But if you do, then receive me just as you would a fool, so that I may do a little boasting. In this self-confident boasting I am not talking as the Lord would, but as a fool. Since many are boasting in the way the world does, I too will boast. You gladly put up with fools since you are so wise! In fact, you even put up with anyone who enslaves you or exploits you or takes advantage of you or pushes himself forward or slaps you in the face. To my shame I admit that we were too weak for that!

What anyone else dares to boast about—I am speaking as a fool—I also dare to boast about. Are they Hebrews? So am I. Are they Israelites? So am I. Are they Abraham's descendants? So am I. Are they servants of Christ? (I am out of my mind to talk like this.) I am more. I have worked much harder, been in prison more frequently, been flogged more severely, and been exposed to death again and again. Five times I received from the Jews the forty lashes minus one. Three times I was beaten with rods, once I was stoned, three times I was shipwrecked, I spent a night and a day in the open sea, I have been constantly on the move. I have been in danger from rivers, in danger from bandits, in danger from my own countrymen, in danger from Gentiles; in danger in the city, in danger in the country, in danger at sea; and in danger from false brothers. I have labored and toiled and have often gone without sleep; I have known hunger and thirst and have often gone without food; I have been cold and naked. Besides everything else, I face daily the pressure of my concern for all the churches. Who is weak, and I do not feel weak? Who is led into sin, and I do not inwardly burn?

If I must boast, I will boast of the things that show my weakness. The God and Father of the Lord Jesus, who is to be praised forever, knows that I am not lying. In Damascus the governor under King Aretas had the city of the Damascenes guarded in order to arrest me. But I was lowered in a basket from a window in the wall and slipped through his hands.

Questions for Personal Reflection

1. In what ways has God's presence protected you?

2. What does God's past protection say to you about his future protection?

Day 7: Group Discussion

The following questions should take about forty-five minutes to answer and discuss. Each member should answer the first question, leaving the remaining questions open-ended. Everyone need not answer, but be sure all members participate.

1. *What are the purposes of God that serve as daily motivation for you?*

2. *Why is being patient such a drain for many believers?*

3.   *When you consider your mortality, what thoughts come to mind?*

4.   *Are we more concerned with being effective where we are or in escaping where we are? How does this affect our spiritual lives?*

5.   *How does waiting on God strengthen our relationship with him?*

6.   *How can your history with God serve as a reminder to be patient with him?*

ENDNOTES

1. William Wordsworth, "Composed upon Westminster Bridge", The Collected Poems of William Wordsworth, (Hertfordshire, United Kingdom: Wordsworth Editions Ltd.), 320.

2. John Bunyan, taken from The Book of Jesus, (New York, NY: Simon & Schuster, 1996), 236–37.

3. François Fénelon, as quoted in The Book of Jesus, edited by Calvin Miller, (New York, NY: Simon & Schuster, 1996), 337.

4. Joseph Bayley, as quoted in The Book of Jesus, edited by Calvin Miller, (New York, NY: Simon & Schuster, 1996), 239–40.

PRAYER JOURNAL

Use the following pages to record both prayer requests and answers.

PRAYER JOURNAL